Frosty and the Christmas Prayer

Based on a True Story
B. W. Reads

Covenant Heritage Press

To my children and grandchildren.
You're all my favorites.

Frosty and the Christmas Prayer
Copyright © 2024 by B. W. Reads

Published by Covenant Heritage Press LLC
CovenantHeritagePress.com

Originally published by Arete Publishing LLC
First Covenant Heritage Press Edition, 2026

ISBN 978-1-964118-00-0

All rights reserved. No part of this book may be reproduced in any form, or by any means electronic or mechanical, including photocopying, recording, or by any information storage or retrieval system, without written permission of the publisher, except in the case of brief quotations in articles and reviews, or as provided by USA copyright law.

Frosty was not just any pet. He was a cherished member of a family with four children: Nellie, Annie, Franklin, and Susan. Each child had a unique bond with the cat, making him a big part of their lives.

With a small patch of white fur accenting his otherwise long black hair, Frosty was a striking fellow! His unique appearance reflected his playful and adventurous personality.

Although he enjoyed life inside the house, Frosty loved going outdoors to explore and play with the neighborhood children. They often could find him perched on the lowest branch of a tree or sitting on the patio, always ready for a new adventure.

More than anything, he liked to catch mice, snakes, birds, chipmunks, and other small creatures that crossed his path.

But catching small animals was challenging for the fluffy cat.

The children's mom and dad placed a lovely collar with bells around his neck to warn nearby animals of his presence.

Everyone thought the small woodland creatures would be safe.

However, those bells didn't deter Frosty. He wore them as a badge of honor. They taught him how to hunt very quietly.

His keen senses and swift reflexes allowed him to easily navigate the wilderness.

He could even walk while crouching low to the ground without making a sound. What a clever cat!

One day, when Frosty was no longer a kitten but still young in years, he went outside as usual, this time on a cold and snowy morning a few weeks before Christmas.

He typically returned home in time for supper, but today was different.

Nobody saw him for the rest of the evening.

When Franklin opened the back door to let him in as usual, Frosty wasn't there.

His absence didn't feel right. Most of the time, he would run inside before the door was fully open.

As the hours passed and Frosty did not return, a sense of unease began to settle over the household. Where could he be?

When he didn't show up the following morning, Franklin went outside and shouted at the top of his voice, calling:

"Frosty! Where are you? Frosty!"

He then listened intently, hoping to hear a meow. But only the wind blowing through a row of pine trees could be heard.

Later that afternoon, after getting off the school bus, Franklin called out for the missing cat during his short walk home, shouting as loudly as he could:

"Frosty! Here kitty kitty!"

"Frosty! Please come home!"

But again, there was no response.

Back at the house, all three girls were consumed with worry. Mom and Dad, their faces etched with concern, tried to hide their own anxiety. Frosty had never been gone this long. The house felt empty without his playful presence.

The family, bundled up in winter coats, combed through the neighborhood, calling out Frosty's name. Despite searching every hiding spot Frosty loved, he was nowhere to be found.

Later that evening, Franklin and Susan searched the entire neighborhood. But once again, there was no sign of Frosty.

The thought of him not returning filled them with a deep sadness.

However, they refused to give up, clinging to the hope that their beloved pet would return.

At that moment, Franklin climbed the stairs to his room, knelt beside the bed, and did what he knew he should have done in the first place. He prayed:

"Dear God, Please bring Frosty back to our family. It's Christmas time, and we all miss him. I'll gladly give up all my Christmas presents to have Frosty back home."

The following morning, Franklin went outside for one more search. Frosty had been missing for almost a whole week. Would he ever come back?

As he walked around the yard, Franklin thought about his prayer. He knew that God might say "no" to his request. But sometimes, God asks us to wait for His perfect timing.

After looking everywhere he could think of, Franklin grew despondent. Sorrow gripped his heart, leading him to despair.

The past week had caused him to lose hope of seeing Frosty again.

He turned around and slowly started walking back to the house . . . but then he heard something.

The sound was quiet.

He stopped and turned around, looking intently across the yard.

And then he heard it again . . . a weak meow.

A weak meow!

Then he heard something else: the sound of collar bells . . . and a second meow.

They were the most beautiful and wonderful sounds he had ever heard!

Franklin was thrilled as he ran back and forth through the snow, trying to locate exactly where the sounds were coming from.

Finally, he saw a skinny animal with long hair and white fur on its chest. It stood on only three legs, the fourth leg obviously wounded. Yet, there was a glimmer of resilience in its eyes. It was Frosty!

Franklin ran to the injured pet, his heart bursting with emotion. Overwhelmed with excitement and relief, he scooped him up, cradled him in his arms, and hurried back to the house, shouting all the way, "Frosty's home! Frosty's home!"

Hearing all the commotion, Franklin's dad ran outside and gently lifted Frosty from Franklin's grip.

The thin, starving cat was in terrible shape.

Both father and son ran back to the house, their hearts filled with joy and worry. Everyone was excited about Frosty's return but shocked at his frail and ragged appearance.

His once sleek black fur was matted and dirty, his body thin and weak. Seeing their beloved pet in such a state strengthened their resolve to nurse him back to health.

"We need to get Frosty to the vet," Franklin's dad said quietly.

He then drove the injured cat to the doctor while Mom held Frosty on her lap.

Everyone back home waited for news about their furry companion. Finally, a few hours later, Mom and Dad walked through the door. In their arms was a purring Frosty wrapped in a warm blanket.

The room erupted with cheers and tears of relief. Frosty was home, safe and sound, just in time for Christmas! His paw was broken, and his ribs were showing, but the doctor said he should get well.

Franklin and his family never found out what caused Frosty's injury or why he went missing for such a long time.

Some people believe he stepped into an animal trap and was later freed. Others thought he may have gotten into a fight with a stray cat. Regardless of what happened, everyone was truly grateful to have him back home again.

But the story doesn't end here. Franklin still had some business to take care of.

He went to his room again, knelt beside the bed, and thanked God for bringing Frosty home.

His heart was filled with gratitude and love for his cherished pet, and he vowed to treasure every moment with him.

A few days later on Christmas morning, Franklin remembered his prayer as he ran down the stairs to the living room.

He didn't know what to expect under the tree.

When he peeked around the corner . . .

. . . he saw several gifts with his name on them!

But his favorite gift of all was Frosty sleeping under the tree. It was the most wonderful answer to a Christmas prayer.

Photograph of Frosty (1965-1981)
under the Christmas Tree